Community Helpers

School Bus Drivers

by Dee Ready

Content Consultant:
Karen E. Finkel, Executive Director
National School Transportation Association

Bridgestone Books
an imprint of Capstone Press

Bridgestone Books are published by Capstone Press
818 North Willow Street, Mankato, Minnesota 56001
http://www.capstone-press.com

Library of Congress Cataloging-in-Publication Data
Ready, Dee.
    School bus drivers/Dee Ready.
    p. cm.--(Community helpers)
    Includes bibliographical references and index.
    Summary: Explains the dress, tools, training, and work of school bus drivers as well as
    special features of their buses.
    ISBN 1-56065-560-7
    1. Bus drivers--Juvenile literature. 2. Bus driving--Vocational guidance--Juvenile
    literature. [1. Bus drivers. 2. School buses. 3. Occupations.]
    I. Title. II. Series: Community helpers (Mankato, Minn.)
HD8039.M8R43   1998
371.8'72--dc21

                                        97-2957
                                          CIP
                                          AC

Photo credits
International Stock/Rae Russel, 18
Maguire PhotoGraFX, cover, 6, 8, 14
Unicorn Stock/Andre Jenny, 4; Jean Higgins, 10; Daniel Olson, 12;
   C. Boylan, 16; Tom McCarthy, 20

Table of Contents

School Bus Drivers

School bus drivers take children to and from school. They stop at bus stops. A bus stop is a place where people wait for buses. Sometimes school bus drivers drive buses for school trips, too.

What School Bus Drivers Do

School bus drivers must drive buses safely. They are careful on the road. They look for trains at train crossings. They make sure children get on and off their buses safely.

What School Bus Drivers Wear

Some school bus drivers wear uniforms. Others wear their own clothes. Some drivers wear jackets to keep warm.

Tools School Bus Drivers Use

School bus drivers use a red stop sign. They also use flashing red lights. The lights and stop sign are parts of the bus. They tell other drivers to stop. This is so children can enter or leave the bus safely.

What School Bus Drivers Drive

School bus drivers drive school buses. A school bus has two rows of seats. It has a walkway between the rows. A school bus can carry many children.

School Bus Drivers and School

School bus drivers take classes to learn driving rules. They learn about the parts of buses. They practice driving buses. Then they take a test to become bus drivers.

Where School Bus Drivers Work

School bus drivers drive buses in all communities. They drive buses in cities and in towns. They drive them in the country, too.

People Who Help School Bus Drivers
Dispatchers help school bus drivers. A dispatcher is someone who talks to drivers over a radio. Some people fix buses. Other people wash buses that are dirty.

School Bus Drivers Help Others

School bus drivers help the community. They drive children to school. They also help children get home safely.

Hands On: Make a Stop Sign

A school bus has a swinging red stop sign on it. The sign tells other drivers to stop. Children can enter and leave a bus safely when cars are stopped. You can make your own stop sign.

What You Need

Cardboard

Red and white crayons

Ruler or stick

Tape

What You Do

1. Ask a grown-up to help you cut the cardboard. Cut it into an eight-sided shape like this picture.
2. Print the word STOP in the middle of the shape. Print it in block letters like this: STOP.
3. Use the white crayon to color in the letters.
4. Color the rest of the sign red.
5. Ask a grown-up for a ruler or stick. Tape it to the back of the sign. This will be the sign's handle.
6. You can use your sign to play school bus.

Words to Know

bus stop (BUHSS STOP)—a place where people wait for buses

community (kuh-MEW-nuh-tee)—a group of people who live in the same area

dispatcher (diss-PACH-er)—someone who talks to bus drivers over a radio

stop sign (STOP SINE)—a red, eight-sided sign that warns other drivers to stop

Read More

Crews, Donald. *School Bus.* New York: Greenwillow Books, 1991.
Denslow, Sharon Phillips. *Bus Riders.* New York: Four Winds Press, 1993.
Ready, Dee. *School Buses.* Mankato, Minn.: Bridgestone Books, 1998.

Internet Sites

Shantz Coach Lines
http://www.shantz-coach.com
School Bus Safety Tips
http://www.skyenet.net:80/fox28/bus.html

Index

DATE DUE

FEB 1 5 2003	OCT 2 1 2002
	OCT 2 5 2002
MAR 1 7 2005	NOV 1 4 2014
APR 1 _ 2005	NOV 2 0 2019
NOV 2 9 2005	
SEP 1 8 2014	MAR 3 0 2024
OCT 0 8 2014	
MAR 1 4 2017	
OCT 0 4 2018	

DEMCO, INC. 38-2931